THE STORY OF
GUERNSEY

This is the story of the Bailiwick of Guernsey - how the islands were formed, how they have been affected by the tides of history and what explains the many monuments that dot the island and the collections of art and objects in its museums.

The Bailiwick of Guernsey is a group of islands located in the English Channel just off the coast of Normandy. It is called a Bailiwick as it is within the jurisdiction of a Bailiff appointed by the King or Queen of England. Guernsey, Alderney and Sark are the largest islands, but Herm, Jethou and Brecqhou are also inhabited. Jersey is the largest of the Channel Islands but is a separate Bailiwick with its own government. Guernsey has an area of just 24 square miles and in the year 2000 had a population around 62,000.

Guernsey is not part of the United Kingdom, so has its own government and its own laws. It is not truly 'independent' however and is a 'Crown Dependency' with the Queen being Head of State. Guernsey has fiercely defended its right to govern its own affairs and did not become a member of the European Union when the UK joined in 1973, enjoying instead a special status under Protocol 3 of the British treaty of accession. English only became the official language of the Islands in the 1920's. Before that it was French and some people on the island still speak local versions of Norman French.

Some 400 generations of people have lived here since the islands became habitable. Guernsey is a unique place, neither English nor French. By exploiting the accidents of history and geography, it has become wealthy whereas many islands are poor. Castles and fortifications point to a turbulent past, but modern Guernsey is peaceful and secure, attracting not only tourists but many international banks and finance companies. How it became this way is the subject of this book.

Written by: **Dr. Jason Monaghan**

Designed & produced by: **Guernsey Museums & Galleries**
Illustrations by: **Brian Byron**

© **States of Guernsey 2010**

Source: VisitGuernsey

Cover image: Detail from a British Rail tourist poster, 1958. © National Railway Museum/SSPL

THE MAKING OF THE ISLANDS

The Channel Islands were not always islands. Guernsey's major rocks were born deep beneath volcanoes then crushed, twisted and cracked deep in the earth. The earliest rocks visible today are up to 2,600,000,000 years old and some of the oldest form the cliffs of the South Coast.

Around 400 to 500 million years ago, Guernsey was at the foot of a mountain range in almost desert-like conditions. Sandstone rocks in the north of Alderney are made from material that washed down from these mountains. Rocks of this age and from the age of the dinosaurs have been completely eroded away in Guernsey, so their fossils are not found here. When dinosaurs walked the earth 300 to 65 million years ago we were close to the coast of the Atlantic Ocean which was only just forming at that time.

Some 5 to 10 million years ago Guernsey was on the sea bed, which explains why the top of the island around the airport and the top of Sark is so flat. Since then, this part of the Earth's crust has risen upwards, pushing the old sea bed 90 metres above the current sea level. Guernsey became an island, and both sea and weather sculpted the land into the shapes we see today.

During the past two to three million years the world has been gripped by ice ages. A fall in temperature across the globe resulted in great sheets of ice spreading out from the Arctic. At times, ice covered most of Britain and was up to 1.5 kilometres thick. This is fifteen times the height of Guernsey's cliffs. As the ice sheets grew, sea levels fell, leaving the Channel Islands as no more than hills in an arctic plain. Guernsey would have looked more like Finland than the place we know today. From time to time, the world warmed, the ice retreated and the seas came back again. Guernsey was at times as warm as Spain is now and the tooth of an extinct elephant has been found in St Peter Port.

island formation

THE BLACK AREA SHOWS THE LAND MASS THAT EXTENDED OUT FROM WHAT IS NOW THE COAST OF FRANCE. THE CHANNEL ISLANDS ARE SHOWN IN WHI

12,000 YEARS AGO

GUERNSEY

FRANCE

11,000 YEARS AGO

GUERNSEY

FRANCE

You can still see the evidence of
sea level change:

- Castel Church is on top of an ancient cliff
  and the bottom of Rectory Hill was a beach
  180,000 years ago when the sea was 30m
  higher than today.

- At Rocquaine you can still see the beach and
  cliffs from 150,000 years ago when the sea
  was 18m higher than today.

- Beside the causeway to Lihou Island you can
  see an ancient beach from 100,000 years ago
  when the sea was 8m higher than today.

- The steep valleys of the islands were carved
  by rushing meltwater during thaws in the icy
  winters. These even extend under the sea!

- The fertile soil of the islands contains a lot of
  'loess' – fine dust that blew in during the cold
  periods.

It should be remembered that the ice ages
have not ended. We now live in an 'interglacial',
a warm period between ice ages. If sea level
continues to rise, it will make the islands
smaller. One day in the far future it may fall
once more meaning we will once again be
connected to France.

1 Raised beach deposit, L'Eree Headland   2 West Coast of Guernsey

Source: VisitGuernsey

2

10,000 YEARS AGO

GUERNSEY

FRANCE

THE ISLANDS TODAY

GUERNSEY

FRANCE

THE FIRST GUERNSEYMEN

The first humans came from Africa and were only able to live in warmer parts of Europe during the Ice Ages. Each time the ice retreated, they came north to hunt animals such as deer and woolly mammoths. Early humans known as Neanderthals lived in caves in Jersey around a quarter of a million years ago. We have no evidence for them in Guernsey, which would have been just a hill at that time, but Neanderthals probably hunted this far. These people became extinct before modern humans began living here, so are not our ancestors.

The world began to warm up around 11,500 years ago (9,500 BC). Animals of the Ice Age such as the mammoth became extinct and were replaced by species familiar today. For a few thousand years it was warmer than in modern times and Guernsey was surrounded by forest. As the ice melted, the seas rose making Guernsey an island again around 9000 BC. Herm/Jethou became separated from Guernsey before 7000 BC and Herm was later cut off from Jethou. Guernsey eventually became split in two, with the northern part forming a small separate island known as the Clos du Valle. Jersey did not become an island until around 5000 BC. The remains of forests such as those of Vazon Bay represent woodland drowned by the rising sea after 5000 BC.

As Guernsey became an island before Europe had fully warmed up after the Ice Age, it means that many species of plant and animal never made it this far before the seas isolated Guernsey from Europe. So, Guernsey has no toads, moles, squirrels, badgers, foxes or snakes. Rabbits were only introduced here by man. The island is warmer than England however which means that many species of plant and animal are found here but not further north.

Guernsey's earliest inhabitants may have lived on land long drowned by the sea. Just off Jethou is a site which is underwater most of the year. Flint tools have been found here including blades made about 12,000 years ago from a period known as the Upper Palaeolithic. At that date, the sea was about 125 metres lower than it is today and Guernsey was still attached to France. A great river ran where the English Channel now stands.

1 & 2   Upper Palaeolithic flint blade from Jethou, 10,000 BC   3   Le Gardien de Tombeau, Le Déhus (see p.8)

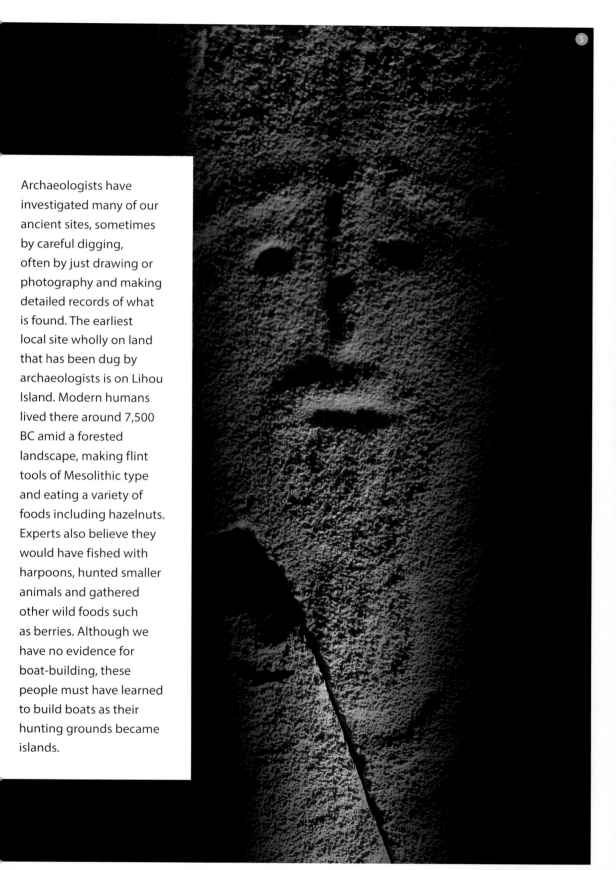

Archaeologists have investigated many of our ancient sites, sometimes by careful digging, often by just drawing or photography and making detailed records of what is found. The earliest local site wholly on land that has been dug by archaeologists is on Lihou Island. Modern humans lived there around 7,500 BC amid a forested landscape, making flint tools of Mesolithic type and eating a variety of foods including hazelnuts. Experts also believe they would have fished with harpoons, hunted smaller animals and gathered other wild foods such as berries. Although we have no evidence for boat-building, these people must have learned to build boats as their hunting grounds became islands.

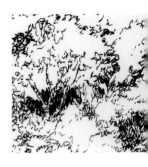

FARMERS OF THE NEOLITHIC

The Neolithic is literally 'the new stone age', when people made flint tools that could be small and sophisticated. We know that fine flint arrowheads were brought here from central France, showing there was a trade taking place across the sea. Sark was a favourite place for making polished stone axes, which are found in Guernsey and further afield. Craftsmen would have made many tools and weapons from wood, antler and bone but few of these survive. Guernsey and Herm would still have been about twice the size they are today when Neolithic cultures took hold in the islands between 5,500 and 5,000 BC.

Humans discovered that crops could be farmed, so started clearing the forest for farmland. Animals were also domesticated and we know by studying the bones of Neolithic people that they were eating dairy products. Farmers could no longer move around in the manner of hunters, so instead they settled in small communities of huts or tents, building pens for their animals and pits to store their crops in. One settlement was on the Camp Varouf opposite Lihou Island. Archaeologists have found another at the bottom of St Julian's Avenue in St Peter Port, taking the history of the district back to at least 5,000 BC. There were also some Mesolithic flints found here, from 2,000 years earlier.

Pottery was another innovation around this time. It was made locally, adopting fashions that were spreading across the Continent. Some pots were also traded between distant tribes. Pottery was important to the early Guernsey people for both cooking and storing food. The first identifiable pottery is in a style called 'Linearbandkeramik' known from continental Europe, showing that either people or ideas were travelling to the islands from the mainland.

1 Barb & Tanged arrowheads, Les Fouaillages   2 Artist's impression of a Neolithic settlement

2

'the new stone age'

THE DOLMEN BUILDERS

Our Neolithic ancestors left behind striking monuments of earth and stone, known locally as dolmens. The earliest is the burial mound of Les Fouaillages, at the edge of L'Ancresse Common. Begun around 4,500 to 4,000 BC, it is older than Stonehenge or the great pyramids of Egypt. Amongst Guernsey's impressive number of monuments are three passage graves dating from between 3,500 to 2,000 BC. Le Déhus is remarkable for the carving on one of the capstones used for its roof known as 'le Gardien de Tombeau' (see p.5). The features of a huntsman can be discerned and it is possible that this figure once stood upright as part of an earlier monument. Whether it represents a real person or some god or spirit, it is the earliest face we have from Guernsey.

The dolmens represent a massive amount of effort, for example one capstone of La Varde weighs around 30 metric tonnes. People with no metal tools, wheels or horses had to pull the great stones uphill and into position. These monuments were clearly very important to the people that built them, even if their exact purpose can no longer be understood. Most of the tombs have their entrance pointing towards the sunrise. Herm has so many tombs in the north of the island that archaeologists have called it an 'Island of the Dead'.

1 La Gran'mere du Chimquiere, St Martins   2 Interior of Déhus Dolmen

'Island of the Dead'

At St Martin's Church is a standing stone carved into the shape of a female figure, known as La Gran'mere du Chimquiere (Grandmother of the cemetery) and there is a second outside the Castel Church. Although these date possibly from 2,500 BC, people still leave offerings of coins or flowers to bring luck – especially if there is a wedding. It is possible that they are the oldest pieces of sculpture in the British Isles.

BRONZE
AGE
GUERNSEY

Archaeologists traditionally divide prehistory into the Stone Ages, Bronze Age and Iron Age, but it is likely that much the same peoples were living in the islands and over the centuries gradually adapted new ideas and new technology. Around 2,000 BC the people of the islands began using bronze, which is a metal made from copper mixed with tin. Neither of these metals was exploited in the islands so would have to be brought here by merchants travelling by ship, possibly from Brittany and Cornwall. A remarkable hoard of bronze was found in Alderney, comprising scrap metal, old axe-heads and spearheads. This would once have belonged to a metalsmith, who had collected the metal so it could be melted down and recycled to make new tools, weapons or brooches. Why the owner never used the metal in the hoard is a mystery. Perhaps it was hidden to stop it being stolen, and the owner died before recovering it. Perhaps it was buried as an offering to a local god. There are several more such hoards from the Channel Islands, mainly from Jersey.

Pottery is very useful to archaeologists as it can survive unchanged for centuries. The shape of a pot and the way it is decorated gives clues to how old it is and what kind of people made it. A particular kind of pottery found on early Bronze Age sites in Guernsey is known, ironically, as the 'Jersey bowl'. Pieces of these bowls were found at the site of the old Royal Hotel, St Julian's Avenue. People were living there at the time the great temples of the Pharaohs were being built in Egypt.

Sea levels had risen by this time to drown the forest at Vazon and Guernsey had reached something like its modern shape. Many old dolmens would have dotted the landscape, and some were still used in religious rituals. Less extravagant Bronze Age burial mounds known as barrows were also built on L'Ancresse Common.

The Bronze Age was the 'heroic' era of the Trojan Wars and the violent stories from the Old Testament of the Bible. Across Europe warfare was becoming widespread and organised. People lived in warrior societies led by armed chieftains. Guernsey people were clearly afraid of attack, probably from across the sea. Ditches were dug and a bank was raised to cut Jerbourg headland off from the rest of the island. This created a refuge large enough to protect hundreds of people and their animals. Remains of these ditches and banks can still be seen in the valley beside the Doyle Column and leading from there to Petit Port.

1   Artist's impression of St Peter Port Bronze Age settlement

'heroic' era

2 Socketed axe head. Would have been mounted on a wooden handle. The lug is for a thong to hold the head tight

3 Spearheads of different sizes and arrowheads are also common

4 Halberd, a dagger shaped blade mounted on a handle and used like a pickaxe

Brian Byron

WARRIORS OF THE IRON AGE

The people known as the Celts originated in Eastern Europe and moved westward in the seven centuries before Christ – or at least their ideas moved this way. The technology for working iron also came westward and was seen in Guernsey by around 700-600 BC. Celtic languages grew into modern Welsh, Breton and Gaelic. A style of Celtic art and design known as 'Late la Tène' can be seen in objects found in Guernsey.

Modern Brittany and most of Normandy was known in the late Iron Age as Armorica and one tribe living there was called the Coriosolites. People called the Osimii inhabited western Brittany, whilst opposite Alderney lived the Venelli. Guernsey appears to have become a stopping point on the trade route bringing wine up the Atlantic coast from Spain and the Mediterranean to Britain. This trade may have been controlled by another tribe called the Veneti. It is possible that the islanders also belonged to one of these tribes.

One of the earliest local Iron Age sites is a settlement on Longis Common, Alderney where pottery was being made. A small late Iron Age settlement at Les Tranquesous in St Saviour's is dated to 150 BC to AD 50, but Guernsey's most exciting site is at King's Road,

beside Acorn House School. A round house was excavated here, in addition to a small cemetery. This included three men buried with long iron swords at their sides and a woman with fine bronze circlets around her neck and arm. Warrior burials of this kind are found at a dozen other sites in Guernsey and could be of important leaders or chieftains. Sadly we do not know the names of any of these people. No warrior burials have been found in Jersey, which may mean that Guernsey was more important at this time, or was inhabited by a tribe with a different way of burying their dead. Ancient writers tell us that the Celts were ruled by warriors who loved wine, feasting and giving fine gifts to their friends and guests. Poets and singers would tell stories of gods and heroes undergoing fantastic adventures. We also hear of the mysterious Druids who acted as priests and judges and we believe that their holy places included springs and woodland groves.

The fortifications at Jerbourg continued to be used and were rebuilt and repaired several times during the Iron Age. The site of the later Vale Castle may have been turned into a hill fort to protect those living in the north of the island. The people of Guernsey also made salt by boiling sea water at several places along the coast. Evidence for this was found in excavations under the Markets in St Peter Port. Many silver Celtic coins have been found in Jersey, but they are very rare in Guernsey. An important hoard of Iron Age silverware was found in Sark during the eighteenth century but has since vanished.

2

Iron Age France is part of the area the Romans knew as Gaul. Archaeologists have found pieces of Roman wine amphorae in excavations, showing that merchants were bringing wine to the islands after about 125 BC. The Roman navy and Roman armies were soon to follow.

the Guernsey warrior

2

LISIA
IN THE
ROMAN EMPIRE

In the first century before Christ was born, the Iron Age tribes in Gaul came under attack from the Roman legions. In 56 BC, the Roman general Julius Caesar defeated the Veneti in a sea battle, whilst on land his General Sabinus defeated the Coriosolites and the other Armorican tribes. After eight years of violent warfare, all of Gaul was conquered by the Romans and it is likely that Guernsey also became part of their Empire around the same time.

We believe that the Romans called Guernsey 'Lisia', but life in the islands would have continued much as it did before we became part of the Empire. A small town grew up in St Peter Port, although we do not know what it was called. Archaeologists have found stone Roman buildings at La Plaiderie and underneath the Markets. Out in the countryside, there may have been a large house, villa or even a fort near the Castel Church, which has Roman tile built into its walls. Roman buildings also lie beneath the sand at Longy Common in Alderney.

Roman merchant ships sailed north from the Mediterranean, from western Gaul and Iberia (Spain) bringing cargoes to northern Gaul, Britain and Germany. Ancient sailors preferred to sail within sight of land, so Lisia was a good place to aim for and provided a sheltered harbour with fresh water. The salt that was made here would have been valuable for preserving food on long voyages.

Some of the cargo would be sold or exchanged in the town, including Roman style pottery and fine goods. Large storage jars known as

1

1 Intaglio, probably from a Roman ring, found in St Peter Port

2 Roman Amphorae found on a Roman wreck off St Peter Port

3 Artist's impression of Roman St Peter Port

3

amphorae have been found that once carried wine, olive oil, fish sauce and other expensive foods. A Roman ship caught fire in the harbour around AD 280 and sank. The wreck was raised by divers between 1984 and 1986 and its timbers preserved. At least one further Roman ship is known to have sunk in the Little Russel, a short distance out from the harbour.

There is no evidence yet that Roman soldiers were ever stationed in Guernsey. It has been said that the building known as 'The Nunnery' in Alderney was originally a Roman fort, but this has not been proved. During the third and fourth centuries AD Britain and Gaul came under attack by pirates and 'barbarian' raiders including the Saxons and the Franks. It became difficult for the Roman Emperor to keep control and in AD 410, the Emperor decided to abandon Britain and not defend it any more. Gaul became a battleground between official Roman armies, rebel Roman generals and barbarian tribes.

Brian Byron

THE GREEN ISLAND

The period after the Romans abandoned Britain is often known as 'the Dark Ages' because so little is known about what happened. The Roman army, their money, pottery and art were gone and their towns and grand buildings fell into ruin. There is very little evidence to tell us what Guernsey was like in the six hundred years after AD 400. The British people fought many wars against the Saxons and some fled to live in Brittany where they came to be called Bretons. Guernsey may have been part of this Breton territory, which was at first still allied to Rome. By AD 486 however, most of Gaul had been captured by the Franks, from where we get the modern name 'France'.

We do not know whether the Bretons or the Franks controlled the islands after they took Gaul from the Romans. Their kings frequently fought amongst themselves for power, so it is possible that the islands changed hands more than once. The Merovingian dynasty of Franks ruled until around 751 when they were overthrown by the Carolingian dynasty, whose most famous king was Charlemagne. In 867 the islands were given to Salomon, the King of the Bretons.

Christian missionaries had been active in the Channel Islands since perhaps the fourth century. A Christian priest named Samson fled Saxon attacks against Wales and found safety at Dol in Brittany. Samson later came to Guernsey and is traditionally said to have founded a chapel close to where he landed, perhaps around AD 560. St Sampson's church may be on or near this site. At this time the island is reported to have had a bountiful corn harvest and a harbour busy with ships.

The Life of St Magloire says that Sark and part of Guernsey were owned by a nobleman called Nivo. St Magloire travelled with St Samson and founded a monastery in Sark and a chapel in the Vale. The mysterious St Tugual may have visited Herm, where a chapel to his (or her) memory now stands.

There are stories of a great flood by the sea in 709 and even an earthquake in 842. More certain is that the region came under attack from 'Northmen', the Vikings, who the locals later called 'Sarazins'. Vikings destroyed St Magloire's cell around 850. They are said to have built a 'castle' in the centre of Guernsey, known as 'Le Chastel du Grand Jeffroi' and probably used the island as a base for raiding France. This 'castle' may have stood near to where the church of Ste Marie du Castel now stands, and may explain the parish name.

1 Possible Viking gaming counter, ninth century, found at Cobo Longhouse

the dark ages

Few ordinary houses are known from this whole period, a lonely exception being the 'longhouse' dating perhaps to the 10th century discovered at Cobo. Around 1034, the island of Jethou was owned by one Restaud who had served as helmsman to Duke Robert the Magnificent, Duke of Normandy 1027-35.

It is thought that the names Guernsey, Jersey and Aurigny (Alderney) date from this period. The ending "-ey" has Scandinavian origins and "groenn" means green. So, the Viking name for Guernsey may have meant "Green Island" or possibly "Green-cornered island" referring to its triangular shape. There are however at least half a dozen alternate theories about the origin of the name.

1

THE DUKES OF NORMANDY

1
Musée de Normandie

Rollo was one of several Viking chiefs who led raids into France in the late ninth and early tenth centuries. Probably in the year 911, the French king made peace with Rollo and his 'Northmen', giving away land that was to form the core of what became known as Normandy. By 933 the Normans had added the Cotentin Peninsula to their lands, and presumably with them the Channel Islands. Even in the 21st century, the islanders are still loyal to the Queen of England, regarding her as the Duke of Normandy (although mainland Normandy was lost in 1204 and the title was surrended to the King of France in 1259).

Possibly worried about Viking attacks on the islands, in about 1020, Duke Richard II gave half the island each to two of his important nobles in the hope they would defend it. He also may have encouraged people to come and live here. The islands were thinly inhabited and many parts of Guernsey were still waste ground, sand dunes or marsh. Very few people lived on the separate island of the Clos du Valle.

The Normans imposed their 'feudal' system upon the islands during the 11th century. Lands were split up into 'fiefs', some retained by the King. The most important person in each fief was the 'Seigneur', who had to perform certain services to the king and sometimes make payments. Ordinary landholders had to pay a number of taxes including such things as Poulage (a property tax paid in chickens), Pannage (a tax on pigs) and Champart (one twelfth of all grain grown). Poulage, which is now only a few pence per year, was until the late 20th century still paid to the Queen on certain properties in Guernsey. At the start of the 21st century a tax on sale of property called Congé was still charged, whilst the Seigneur of Sark held certain powers left over from 'feudal' days.

Norman politics and internal wars meant that ownership of land changed from one noble family to another, and was also held by powerful bishops and Abbeys. In 1066 Duke William II invaded England and after winning the Battle of Hastings he became King William I of England as well as Duke of Normandy.

The English Kings also ruled lands in Gascony, western France, and at this time Guernsey was an important stopping place for ships bringing Gascon wine to England. King Richard I 'The Lionheart' made his brother John 'Lord of the Isles' around 1195-98. Men holding this title, or others known as 'Wardens', would rule the islands in the name of the king for the next few hundred years.

1 Statue of William the Conqueror   2 Artist's impression of a ship unloading its cargo, St Peter Port circa 1150

Brian Byron

1204
AND
ALL THAT

Until the year 1204, Channel Islands life had been tied to what was happening on the nearby French coast. After 1204, it was England that would dominate the islands' history. When Prince John became King, he was embroiled in a war with the King of France, Philippe Auguste. John's armies however suffered defeat in 1204 and the whole of Normandy fell into French hands, apart from the Channel Islands. The French seized the islands temporarily but were driven off.

A mercenary and pirate known as Eustace the Monk was involved in holding Guernsey for England. The true story is however obscured by a medieval novel in which Eustace embarks on adventures reminiscent of Robin Hood. He is said to have pillaged the island mercilessly and he later took the French side in the war against England. His family seem to have been in control of Guernsey for a few years, but were instructed to hand the island back after Eustace was executed by the English in 1217. Henry III of England's right to the islands was finally confirmed in the Treaty of Paris of 1259.

1   Castle Cornet as it may have looked in the 13th century

2   The earliest surviving document in Guernsey is this charter from 1060 telling us there are six churches in Guernsey paying tithes to an Abbey in Normandy. It also contains the first reference to St Peter Port

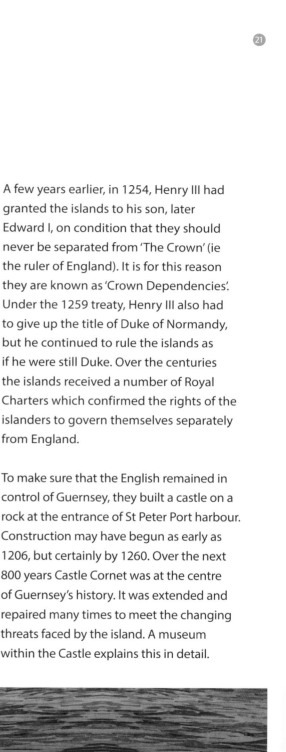

A few years earlier, in 1254, Henry III had granted the islands to his son, later Edward I, on condition that they should never be separated from 'The Crown' (ie the ruler of England). It is for this reason they are known as 'Crown Dependencies'. Under the 1259 treaty, Henry III also had to give up the title of Duke of Normandy, but he continued to rule the islands as if he were still Duke. Over the centuries the islands received a number of Royal Charters which confirmed the rights of the islanders to govern themselves separately from England.

To make sure that the English remained in control of Guernsey, they built a castle on a rock at the entrance of St Peter Port harbour. Construction may have begun as early as 1206, but certainly by 1260. Over the next 800 years Castle Cornet was at the centre of Guernsey's history. It was extended and repaired many times to meet the changing threats faced by the island. A museum within the Castle explains this in detail.

a Crown Dependency

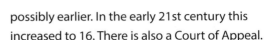

WHO RULES GUERNSEY?

During the Middle Ages we start to see the institutions familiar in Guernsey's modern government appearing.

The Lieutenant Governor is appointed by the English King (or Queen) and was responsible for the defence of Guernsey. The post of 'Lord of the Isles' or 'Warden' used in the Middle Ages came to be known as 'Captain', which was later replaced by 'Governor'. Governors resident in the island would live in Castle Cornet, until it was heavily damaged by an explosion in 1672. When Governors tended not to live here, they would appoint a 'Lieutenant Governor'. No Governor has been in office since 1834 and the Queen's representative on the island is today designated 'Lieutenant Governor'. This post has often been held by a distinguished officer from one or another of the armed services.

The Bailiff is the president of the Royal Court and acts as both the senior judge on the island and the chairman of States' meetings. The Bailiff is today appointed by the English Crown, the office having become distinct from that of sub-warden in the early 14th century.

Jurats judge court cases and today sit in the Royal Court. The island has had twelve Jurats since at least the early 13th century and possibly earlier. In the early 21st century this increased to 16. There is also a Court of Appeal.

The States is the island's parliament, developed from the 'Etats' of leading islanders that began to meet in the fifteenth century. It was originally made up of men such as rectors and parish constables. Since 1899 it has included 'Deputies' elected by the people, but it was not until after 1948 that the States became truly democratic.

Parishes, of which there are ten in Guernsey, are administered by Constables. With regard to local matters these act with the Douzaine of twelve people elected by parishioners, which is like a 'parish council'.

For most years between 1275 and 1328, the islands were under the power of a Burgundian knight called Otto de Grandison. He is celebrated by a statue on the South Esplanade, despite being perhaps the greatest villain in Guernsey's history. He was made Lord of the Isles, but only came here once. De Grandison used his power to extract money from the islands by any means he could find, causing a series of disputes with the Jurats, Bailiffs and Seigneurs. One of his officials was the infamous Gautier de la Salle, who was hanged for murder.

1   Model of a mangonel as used in Castle Cornet, 14th Century

2   Medieval coins from Albecq, c.1375

3   The English retake Castle Cornet, 1345

The French raided the islands in 1294, burning St Peter Port and killing the Bailiff and about 1,500 people. In 1336 and 1337 the French attacked again. Soon after the Hundred Years War began in 1338, the French managed to capture Castle Cornet, and so take control of Guernsey. English forces led by Walter de Weston took the island back in 1340, but Castle Cornet remained in French hands until finally recaptured by Geoffrey de Harcourt in 1345. The castle fell again in 1356 but this time was swiftly retaken, with the help of a force of Jerseymen. The Guernsey Militia was formed around 1331 as a force of local men assembled to defend the island in times of need, though as early as the reign of John some sort of local force appears to have been organised.

Constantly under threat, Guernsey was fortified further. Castles of refuge allowed people to find safety during French attacks. One at Ivy Castle is known from 1244 and another at Jerbourg was in existence by 1309 (although this cannot now be seen). It is not thought that St Peter Port was surrounded by a wall, but in 1357 La Tour Beauregard was built on the place now known as Tower Hill. A second tower, Le Tourgand, was built in the Pollet which was then the northernmost edge of town.

Owen of Wales, acting with French support, landed at Vazon in 1372. His army defeated hastily assembled Guernsey forces near where the Castel School now stands. He then attacked La Tour Beauregard but was unable to capture Castle Cornet. He withdrew to France after causing much damage and suffering. A folk legend has also grown up around the battle in which the invaders came from the land of the fairies to steal the Guernsey women. The Constable of France launched further attacks on the islands in 1373 and in 1380 the French seized temporary control of Castle Cornet. A coin hoard buried at Albecq around 1375 and not recovered by its owner shows that the Guernsey folk lived in fear of attack. Wars and raids continued over the next century.

LIFE IN MEDIAEVAL GUERNSEY

Guernsey's ten parishes may be very ancient. Both the Town Church and Castel Church stand close to Roman ruins, whilst there may have been a chapel at St Sampson's since the sixth century. Each parish appears to have had a church by the eleventh century and the current Town Church is first referred to by name in a document dating to the 1050's as 'Sancti Petri de Portu'. The Castel church contains the remains of mediaeval wall paintings. More wall paintings depicting the last supper survive in the single-roomed chantry chapel dedicated to Ste Apolline which was founded under charters dated 1392 and 1394. Parish churches were supported partly by the Abbeys in France, but mostly by local people who had to contribute to the 'Tresors' of each church. Church services were in Latin, although the people of the islands spoke a version of Norman French.

The Church played an important part in the Mediaeval life of the islands and from time to time large areas of the islands were owned by one or another religious house. The Bishop of Coutanches owned a fief. Benedictine Monks from the Abbey of Mont St Michel built a Priory next to the Vale Church, the remains of which have all but vanished. The Benedictines also founded the Priory of Notre Dame on

1 The Last Supper, depicted at Ste Apolline's Chapel

2 Priory of Notre Dame, Lihou Island, as it may have looked in the 14th Century

Lihou Island, perhaps in 1156. Like much of the other ecclesiastical property, the priory stayed in French hands until the late fourteenth or early fifteenth century. The ruins have been excavated by archaeologists and can still be visited. A Franciscan friary was established in the grounds where Elizabeth College now stands, visible now only in a few pieces of stonework and the name of La Rue des Frères. Land held by the religious houses was eventually seized by the English kings.

Merchants lived in St Peter Port, which remained an important harbour. A group of mediaeval shipwrecks just inside the harbour mouth may have sunk in a storm or in one of the wars. Fishermen mainly caught conger eels, which were hung up to dry at 'éperqueries' and salted at 'saleries' before being packed into barrels and sold abroad.

Ordinary farming folk were mostly poor and made extra money by using English wool to knit clothes, hats and especially socks. By the sixteenth century, even Queen Elizabeth's household were wearing Guernsey stockings.

The Black Death struck the island severely in 1348, so much so that Royal revenues could not be collected. Sark seems to have been left virtually uninhabited following all the wars and French raids. It gained a reputation for being a pirate's lair. A respite from French attacks came at last when it was agreed that the islands would be neutral in times of war between England and France and ships would be safe in Channel Islands' waters. This was confirmed by a 'Bull' issued by Pope Sixtus IV in 1481 and gave Guernsey two hundred years of relative peace.

Brian Byron

REFORMATION
AND
HERESY

The sixteenth century was a dangerous time in Europe. The dominance of the Roman Catholic Church was challenged by Protestants, leading to wars, murders and massacres. England began to break away from the Church of Rome when Henry VIII divorced his first wife. The English 'Reformation' was a consequence of this. Norman Franciscan friars were expelled from Guernsey in 1536 on the orders of Thomas Cromwell, Henry VIII's reforming minister. In 1569, even the powerful Bishop of Coutances lost his interests in the islands. Guernsey came under the Bishop of Winchester from 1568/9.

When the Catholic Queen Mary came to the throne of England, she was keen to stamp out Protestant ideas and many people were executed for their beliefs. Such terrors even reached Guernsey.

In 1556, Catherine Cauchés and her daughters Perotine Massey and Guillemine Guilbert were thrown into prison in Castle Cornet when Perotine was suspected of stealing. The Bailiff Helier Gosselin and the 12 Jurats found the women innocent of theft, but during the investigation neighbours alleged that the three had not been attending Church. They were tried again, this time by the Dean Jacques Amy and the Ecclesiastical Court, who found them guilty of heresy. The Bailiff and Jurats then condemned the women to death. On 17th July the women were led to Tower Hill, strangled, then burned alive. In a horrible scene, Perotine gave birth to a baby boy as she died and this baby too was thrown onto the fire.

The story is found in Foxe's Book of Martyrs which is on show in Guernsey Museum and features on the Guernsey Millennium Tapestry at St James.

After the Protestant Queen Elizabeth I came to the throne, those involved in the deaths were put on trial themselves. This did not end terror, as alleged 'witches' were also executed in this period – records survive of the burning of no fewer than 50 people.

French Protestant 'Huguenots' fled to Guernsey to escape the vicious Wars of Religion sweeping France and won the sympathy of the islanders. English Protestants were now able to hear church services in their own language instead of Latin. In Guernsey, however, the people still spoke Norman French. In consequence, French Calvinists were brought across to preach in the churches. The Calvinists were particularly stern Protestants, imposing severe penalties on people who did not attend church or indulged in frivolous acts such as singing or dancing in public.

1 The three Cauchés women are taken away during the seige of Castle Cornet

2 The execution of the three Cauchés women, July 1556, as shown in Foxe's Book of Martyrs

burnt at the stake

Catholic Spain and Protestant England were at war from 1585 to 1604, from which we famously remember the defeat of the Spanish Armada in 1588. There were however other Spanish armadas and one fleet set out in 1595 to destroy the Channel Islands, but became lost and burned Mousehole in Cornwall instead. English soldiers came to reinforce our castles and also landed in France to fight the Spanish and French Catholics. On one of these missions, an English ship carrying soldiers and weapons was wrecked off Alderney. Objects found on this wreck by maritime archaeologists can now be seen in Alderney Museum.

Brian Byron

THE ENGLISH CIVIL WARS

The Civil Wars were the result of disagreements between King Charles I and Parliament over how England should be ruled. Warfare broke out in 1642. Some of Guernsey's wealthy landowners were sympathetic to the King. The Lieutenant Governor Sir Peter Osborne had however made himself unpopular in the island, which had also suffered loss of trade due to the King's foreign wars. The island's strong Calvinist movement added to the decision for Guernsey to throw out the Royalist Bailiff and support Parliament. Jersey meantime declared its support for the King.

Castle Cornet was manned by English soldiers and Osborne retreated there, refusing to hand it over to the Island's authorities. Three notable islanders were appointed Parliamentary Commissioners and told to take control of the island. In February 1643, an attack was launched against the castle, but failed. Osborne and about 60 'Royalist' soldiers continued to hold the castle for the King. Parliament laid siege to the castle, but could not stop supplies coming in by sea. Late in 1643, the three Commissioners were lured to a meeting after which they were captured and imprisoned in the castle. They made a daring escape at the end of the year, just as their execution warrant had been received. Osborne was replaced in 1646, but his successors managed to hold out for another six years. During the siege, cannons on shore would occasionally fire at the castle or at Royalist ships and many houses in St Peter Port were damaged by cannon balls when the castle and ships fired back. Attempts to storm the castle came to nought, and in the last attack, the Guernsey Militia lost 30 men killed when they were repulsed.

After King Charles was defeated and executed, the remaining Royalist fortresses in England surrendered one-by-one. Jersey also finally gave up the fight. On 19th December 1651, Castle Cornet was the last of the Royalist strongholds to surrender.

1 Castle Cornet, circa 1670   2 Royalist gunners at Castle Cornet fire on St Peter Port   3 Helmet used during the English Civil War

After the restoration of Charles II as King of England in 1660, troops were sent to the island to enforce the official Anglican form of church worship. Calvinist attitudes in the island gradually faded away over the next two hundred years. The century still had more drama in store, however. Castle Cornet was struck by lightning in 1672, exploding its gunpowder stocks and killing the Governor's wife and mother. The great donjon (keep) was destroyed, leaving the castle as the low squat shape we see today.

3

2

Brian Byron

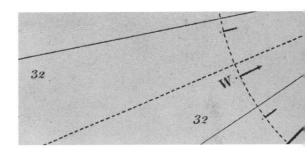

PRIVATEERS AND SMUGGLERS

The neutrality of the Islands ended in the reign of William III in 1689 and Guernsey ship owners began attacking merchant ships of France and other enemies of England. Armed with 'letters of marque' from the English king, these 'privateers' made good profits from what was virtually legalised piracy. The fortunes of several island families were made this way during wartime. In 1692, privateer John Tupper of Guernsey sighted a French fleet assembling to support the claim of James II to the English throne. He alerted the English fleet, then took part in the crushing victory of Cap La Hogue for which he was awarded a gold medal by King William and Queen Mary.

Guernsey privateers grew in force each time there was a war against France, Holland or Spain, with over 100 armed ships being sent out by 1713. Even American ships became fair game after that country rebelled against Britain in 1775. It was not all glory and profit however, as some local ships were sunk and men killed or captured during these adventures.

St Peter Port served as an 'entrepôt' between England and France. Wine and brandy from France, Spain or Portugal would be brought to Guernsey by ship and stored to mature in the cellars of the town. It was later transferred into small casks for collection by merchants who would take it on to England – often 'smuggling' the goods past English revenue-men. English wool was imported under licence and knitted into stockings and the like before being sold in England and Europe. Many island fortunes were built on this trade and on the ship-building and cask-making that went with it. One drawback of this success was that at times so many men were at sea or busy knitting or making casks that the farms went short of workers and the island had to import food.

As long ago as the reign of Queen Elizabeth I, the English government had complained about Guernsey ships continuing to trade with the 'enemy' in times of war. The islanders called this activity 'fair trading' and defended their right to carry it out, despite English attempts to stop what they saw as smuggling. When the English imposed anti-smuggling laws in 1807 it was a blow to the islanders' wealth and many businesses suffered.

The story of Guernsey's adventures with the sea is told in the Maritime Museum at Castle Cornet and in the Fort Grey Shipwreck Museum.

1　Thomas de Sausmarez (1713-1764)

2　Philip de Sausmarez (1710-1747)

These brothers took part in Admiral Anson's voyage around the world in which the treasure-rich Manila Galleon was captured in 1744, beginning that family's famous naval exploits. Philip was later killed fighting the French

3　Privateer in a Storm, attributed to John Brookings

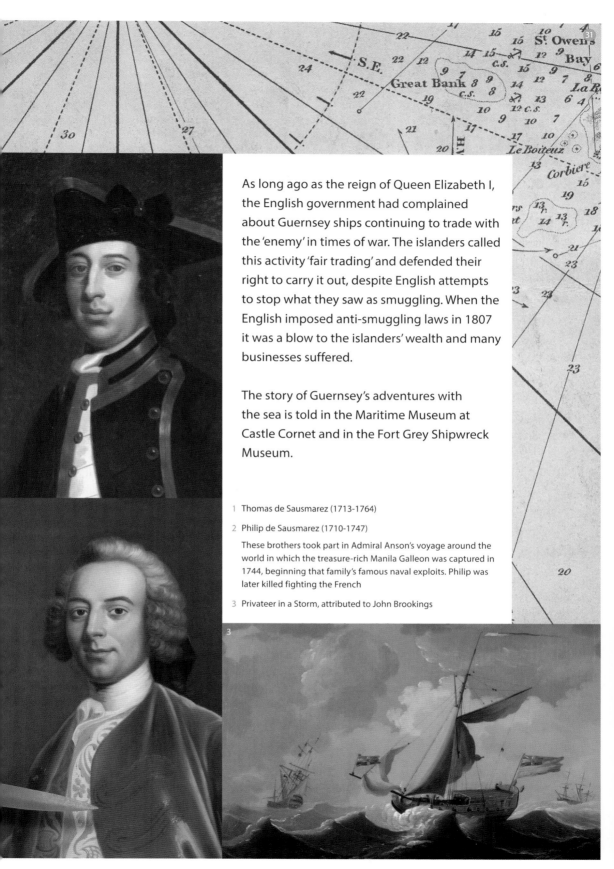

DEFENCES AGAINST THE FRENCH

VisitGuernsey

Throughout the eighteenth century, Great Britain was often at war with France. Confident in its sea power, Britain was shaken by defeats at the hands of the Americans between 1775 and 1781. The French allied with the Americans, leading to fears that the Channel Islands would be invaded, but a French attack on Jersey in 1780 failed dismally. In January 1781 a second invasion led by Baron de Roullecourt was defeated in the short but bloody Battle of Jersey fought out in St Helier's Royal Square. Guernsey privateers were again active against the French, the Americans and their allies.

The greatest Anglo-French struggle followed the French Revolution of 1789. With only a few brief interludes, Britain and France were at war from 1793 to 1815, which put Guernsey in the front line. In 1794, Sir James Saumarez decoyed a French squadron off the west coast of Guernsey, using his Pilot's knowledge of the rocks and reefs to save his ships from capture by the enemy. The Revolutionary Wars turned into the Napoleonic Wars from the date Napoleon Bonaparte became Emperor of France. The threat of invasion from France was ended by Lord Nelson at the Battle of Trafalgar in 1805, where 29 Guernseymen fought on the victorious side.

The islands were progressively refortified in face of the French threat. Regular soldiers from the British army were also stationed in the island, originally based in Castle Cornet. The Castle was no longer suitable for the garrison, however, so a large new base was constructed at Fort George in 1780. This is now a housing development, but the main gate survives and a major outwork can be seen at Clarence Battery.

A series of 15 loopholed towers were constructed in 1778-9, of which twelve still survive. Gun batteries were also built to carry cannon – the best of these can be seen at Rousse and at Mont Chinchon. In addition to the Regulars, the island was also defended by the Royal Guernsey Militia, which all men between 16 and 60 might be required to join. It included over 2,000 men organised into three 'regiments' – North, West and East (Town) - plus an artillery company. A South Regiment and a unit of cavalry were formed later. The militiamen were ordinary farmers and fishermen whilst the island's wealthier men became its officers. Women would often stand guard instead of their husbands or sons who were needed to work the farms. Originally dressed in civilian clothes, the militia were finally given scarlet uniforms in 1782.

1 Mont Chinchon battery   2 General Sir John Doyle, Lieutenant Governor of Guernsey   3 Loophole tower on L'Ancresse Common

2

General Sir John Doyle, the Lieutenant Governor of Guernsey, decided that the islands needed further fortification. In 1804 he organised the construction of three more advanced 'Martello' towers at Fort Grey, Fort Saumarez and Fort Hommet. He was also concerned that the French would seize the Vale, with the troops at Fort George powerless to intervene. Accordingly in 1806-08 he arranged for the tidal Braye du Valle to be reclaimed from the sea and for a straight military road to be built across it. If you travel north along the Route Militaire, the Vale Pond on the left is the last remnant of this channel. St Sampson's waterfront where the old bridge ran across the Braye is still known as 'the Bridge'. Guernsey at last became a single island.

Source: VisitGuernsey

4   5

4   Major General Sir Isaac Brock (1769-1812)
Guernsey born officer credited with saving Canada from an American invasion in 1812. He was killed at the Battle of Queenston Heights

5   Admiral Sir James Saumarez, Baron de Saumarez (1757-1836)
The island's greatest naval hero, who commanded battleships at the Battles of Cape St Vincent, the Nile and Algeciras. He gained great affection in Sweden for his careful diplomacy whilst commanding HMS Victory in the Baltic between 1808 and 1813

PEACE
AND
PROGRESS

After the fall of Napoleon, Guernsey enjoyed 99 years of peace but had to adjust to the rapid pace of progress. The knitting industry which had supplemented the incomes of country folk ceased to be important after the Industrial Revolution brought factories to England. It is from the early nineteenth century however that we first hear of the 'Guernsey' – a tough, warm navy blue woollen sweater still favoured by sailors. This style of jumper had probably been made in the islands since the 15th century.

If the countryside remained relatively poor, St Peter Port became prosperous. The town was still quite small in the early nineteenth century, with narrow alleyways and a few grand houses of the merchants. The Rohais was the main route out of town and the High Street the only other major thoroughfare. Improvements in sanitation and the influx of immigrants from England and Ireland increased the population by 50% by 1850. A 'New Town' was built in the fields where Havilland Street and St John Street now stand. Town was improved by a wave of new building projects. Successful businessmen Guille and Allès gave the island its library and first museum in 1870. Their collection now

1

makes up some of the exhibits on show at Guernsey Museum & Art Gallery. Methodism took strong root in the islands after John Wesley came to preach here in 1787 and the movement grew in strength during the 19th century, with several chapels being built in the islands. The Guernsey Militia remained an important part of island life, with over 3,000 men in its regiments. Service as officers was popular with the island's wealthier men. Militia parades were common sights and red-coated officers added dash to dances and social occasions.

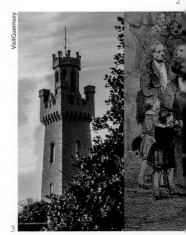

VisitGuernsey

2

3

1 Frederick Corbin Lukis (1788-1871)

Guernsey's best known antiquarian scholar. In 1811 he investigated La Varde dolmen and later excavated the Déhus, founding a small private museum of his finds. His notes and illustrations on the prehistoric sites of the islands are still invaluable to archaeologists today

2 Queen Victoria and Prince Albert visited Guernsey in 1846 and again in 1859

3 To commemorate the first visit Victoria Tower was erected in 1848

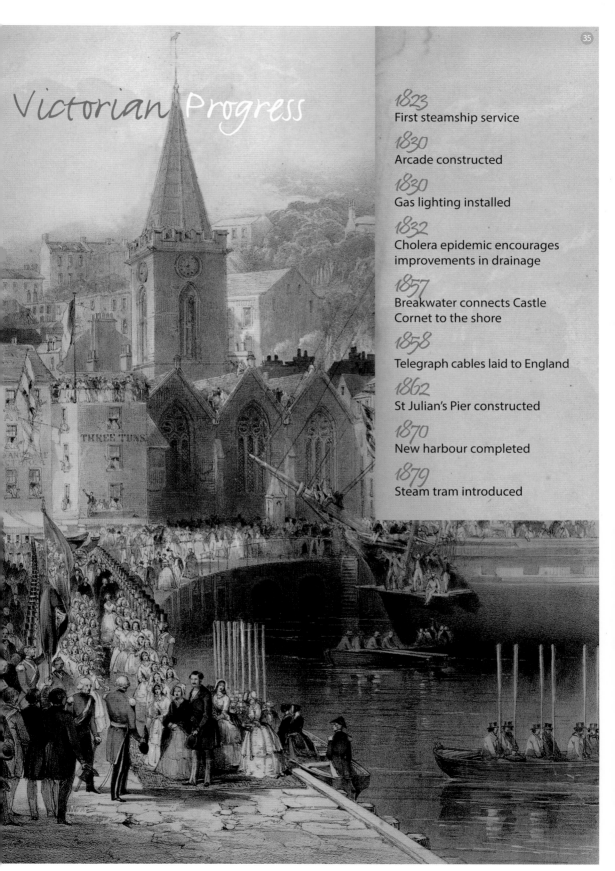

Victorian Progress

1823
First steamship service

1830
Arcade constructed

1830
Gas lighting installed

1832
Cholera epidemic encourages
improvements in drainage

1857
Breakwater connects Castle
Cornet to the shore

1858
Telegraph cables laid to England

1862
St Julian's Pier constructed

1870
New harbour completed

1879
Steam tram introduced

SHIPS AND GRANITE

Fishing has been an occupation of islanders from prehistoric times to the modern day. Many locals still keep a fishing boat even if they have jobs ashore. From the seventeenth to early nineteenth centuries, Guernsey fishermen also caught cod off Newfoundland and dried it to bring back to Europe. Guernsey ships also took part in trade with the cod fisheries. Ships would carry goods needed in North America, exchange these for cod then carry this to Spain and other Catholic countries where fish was eaten on Fridays instead of meat. Fruit and other cargoes were then brought back to the island or to England.

The end of the Napoleonic wars in 1815 caused an economic crisis and unemployment. Peace however allowed merchants to find new markets across the world and within a few years there was a wave of ship-building in Guernsey. Shipyards began at Havelet Bay and ran along the front between St Peter Port and St Sampson's. Some 300 ships were built in the nineteenth century. Guernsey ships carried stone to England and were also used in the coastal trade in other British goods, especially coal. In the second half of the century the wooden sailing ship could not compete with the iron steamer and the ship-building industry quickly came to an end.

Guernsey's stone has been employed since the earliest dolmens were raised. The Blue Granite, or diorite, is an especially good building stone. Quarrying grew apace in the 19th century, with over 200 quarries being active at times. St Sampson's was the main harbour from which this granite was shipped to England where Guernsey granite was used on London Bridge and that from the islet of Crevichon was used in St Paul's Cathedral. Almost half a million tons per year was being quarried by the early twentieth century and the north of island at that time looked very 'industrial'. When the Great War broke out in 1914, Guernseymen were recruited into special quarrying companies of the British army.

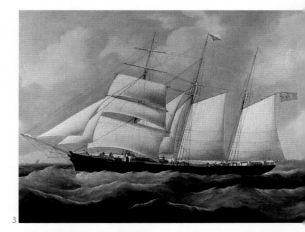

1 William Le Lacheur (1802-1863)
   Guernsey ship owner who established the coffee trade
   with Costa Rica between 1840 and 1860

2 Guernsey quarry workers

3 The ship (barquentine) "Times" owned by William Le Lacheur

GUERNESIAIS – OUR LOCAL LANGUAGE

1

Known as 'Guernsey French' or 'patois' the local language is actually a form of Norman. Old French evolved from the Vulgar Latin spoken in the region when it was part of the Roman Empire. Many different regional languages evolved in France before the modern 'standard' French was agreed. One of these languages was Norman, and it is assumed that it was spoken in the islands a thousand years ago when we were ruled by the Dukes of Normandy.

After the Norman conquest of England in 1066, Norman French became the language used at court and by the nobles. It was three hundred years before 'English' became the official language of England, and by this time a lot of Norman French words had been added to English. In Guernsey however the local people continued speaking Norman. It gradually changed into a distinct local language. Sark, Alderney and Jersey all developed their own variations of Norman.

Guernsey's Royal Court and officials employed 'The King's French' from the late Medieval period to the early 20th century and this was also widely spoken by the merchants and upper classes in the town. When schools were set up, these taught standard French which was referred to as 'The Good French'. English was spoken by the many soldiers stationed here and by British people who moved here to live or work in town. In 1926 English was made an official language of the States, but people of the countryside continued speaking Guernesiais well into the middle of the 20th century. It is primarily a spoken language and there is still debate over how its words are spelled and what its proper grammar is (pronounced Gièrnesiais, you may see it spelled Guernesiaise or Dgernesiais). Words and pronunciations used in the north of the island can differ from those in the west of the island. To those who know French it looks rather strange. The first dictionary was written by Georges Métivier, who with a small number of writers aimed to preserve the language with poems and stories.

The German Occupation of 1940 struck a heavy blow to the language – not only from the attempt to get all islanders speaking German! Many children were evacuated to England and forgot how to speak Guernesiais. Some adults joined the British forces, travelled the world and married non-islanders. After the war, an influx of British settlers, tourists and the influence of radio and television further diluted the language.

1   Self-portrait of Denys Corbet as an artist. He also wrote poems and prose in Guernesiais

2   Georges Métivier (1790-1881)
    wrote the first dictionary of Guernesiais in 1870. He was the island's greatest Romantic poet, writing in the Norman language

2

Some Guernesiais phrases

Bianvnu.
Welcome.

Coume tchi que l'affaire va?
How are things going?

Énn amas bian merci.
Very well thank you.

Quaï temps qu'i fait?
What's the weather like?

I fait caoud ogniet.
It's warm today.

A la perchoïne!
Until next time!

In the year 2000 there were about 1,300 fluent speakers of Guernesiais and perhaps twice this number spoke some phrases. In addition, groups of enthusiasts and government initiatives strive to keep the language alive. Look for Guernsey names on street signs, Guernesiais phrases on restaurant menus, and listen out for special programmes on local radio.

La Victime-Métivier

Veis-tu l's écllaers, os-tu l'tounère?
Lé vent érage et la née a tché!
Les douits saont g'laïs, la gnièt est nère -
Ah, s'tu m'ôimes ouvre l'hus - ch'est mé!

Do you see the lightning, do you hear the thunder?
The wind is raging and the snow has fallen!
The streams are frozen, the night is dark -
Ah, if you love me open the door - it's me!

ARTISTS AND WRITERS

1

The islands have inspired many artists, poets and writers, particularly since the early nineteenth century. Renoir painted here and it is common to see Channel Islands subjects by Wimbush, Kilpack and Octavius Oakley to name a few. Local artists include Blampied and Gosselin and more recently Peter Le Vasseur.

Victor Hugo, the notable French poet and author, was exiled from his native France due to his opposition to Napoleon III. In1855 he came to Guernsey and lived here for 14 years, completing Les Misérables and Les Travailleurs de la Mer amongst other works. His bizarrely decorated home at Hauteville House is today open to the public.

William J Caparne was born in Newark on Trent, but came to live in Guernsey in 1895 after the death of his wife. He depicted the island in soft watercolours or pastels and his love of flowers features in many of his paintings such as 'House of Nerines'. Irises were a particularly favourite subject and he ran a business selling bulbs and seeds.

William A Toplis was born in Sheffield but moved to Sark in 1883 where at times he lived close to poverty. His watercolours and oil paintings of that island include highly detailed depictions of rocks. In 1908, Toplis took prints from 21 of his paintings and in collaboration with author John Oxenham, published the luxurious vellum-bound Book of Sark.

1   Bronze Bust of Victor Hugo by Rodin

2   The Venus Pool, Sark, by William A. Toplis

3   The gathering of vraic in Rocquaine Bay, Guernsey by Peter Le Lievre

2

Peter Le Lievre was born in Guernsey in 1812, became a wine merchant, militia officer and prominent member of Victorian society. He is now remembered for his watercolour paintings which record island landscapes, buildings and people of the era. These are still popular subjects for postcards and prints sold locally.

Paul J Naftel was born in 1817 and lived in Guernsey until he moved to London in 1870. The son of a clock and watchmaker who also sold artists' materials, he became a successful artist and art teacher, having works exhibited in London. In 1846 he recorded Queen Victoria's visit to Guernsey and sent a finished watercolour to the Queen herself. His second wife Isabel was also an artist, as was their daughter Maud.

3

THE GREAT WAR 1914-18

'Diex Aie' - 'God help us'

In August 1914, German troops invaded Belgium and Britain declared war on Germany. The Great War that followed lasted four years and cost millions of lives. Guernsey was loyal to Britain and by November 9% of its young men had volunteered to join the British Army or Royal Navy. Some went to join the French army, who were fighting a bitter battle to halt a German attack that almost reached Paris. By early 1915 the war had become a stalemate and both sides 'dug in', forming two opposing lines of trenches stretching from the English Channel to Switzerland. Guernseymen who volunteered joined the Royal Irish Regiment and Royal Irish Fusiliers. It was joked that Guernseymen were put with the Irish because neither could speak English properly.

1915 and 1916 saw Guernseymen killed and wounded at the terrible battles of Loos and the Somme. In December 1916, it was decided that Guernsey should have its own regiment. The Royal Guernsey Militia was suspended and its men formed into the Royal Guernsey Light Infantry (RGLI). The RGLI fought at the Battle of Cambrai in November 1917, which was a surprise attack on the German defensive lines using masses of the newly invented 'tanks'. The Germans soon recovered from the surprise

and launched a counter-attack, which the Guernsey soldiers helped fight off. Of 1,200 men it sent into the battle, the RGLI lost 120 killed, 250 wounded and another 250 missing. Hardly a family in the island did not know someone who had been killed. The motto of the regiment was 'Diex Aie'; supposedly the Norman battle-cry, it was grimly translated as 'God help us'.

At home, women took over the jobs of men who had joined the army, including working in banks and shops and serving as 'conductorettes' on the trams. Some went to England to work in the factories making weapons. Others volunteered as nurses. Food was in short supply, so a 'Food Control Committee' was set up to make sure everyone had a fair share. The price of coal and many essential foods doubled during the war.

1   Detail of the RGLI colours that now hang in the Town Church

2   Soldiers of the RGLI with the regimental mascot "Joey"

3   Cap badge of the RGLI

4   Private of the Royal Guernsey Light Infantry with his family, 1917

In March 1918, the Germans launched their last great offensive of the war, attempting to smash the exhausted British and French armies. During the Battle of the Aisne, the RGLI were once again called upon to help stop the Germans, but in doing so the regiment was almost destroyed. The few men who remained formed a guard at headquarters for the rest of the war, where they were reviewed by King George V.

After the German attacks failed, armies from the British Empire and America launched an offensive of their own which finally ended the war. An Armistice was signed on 11 November 1918. Guernsey, Alderney and Sark had just over 20,000 men before the war and of these, 5,273 went to fight and 1,172 were killed. Many more were wounded and one family in Sark suffered five sons killed. The names of the fallen are inscribed on the memorials which can be seen in each parish. It was not until the 1930's that the islands' populations returned to the levels seen before the war.

LIVING OFF THE LAND

The people of Guernsey have always been resourceful, often having more than one source of income. A quarryman might keep a cow, a fisherman might grow a few tomatoes, a farmer's wife would knit stockings whilst the farmer would crush apples in a big granite trough to make cider. During the tourist boom, a family might also run a guest house or holiday chalet.

Guernseymen have for many centuries maintained small farms. There are no real villages and few large farms. The shift to horticulture in the nineteenth century partly explains the look of the island where houses are built along the main roads, interspersed with small fields or glasshouses. The land has traditionally been fertilised by spreading 'vraic' (seaweed) on the fields. Much land in the high parishes was once used for growing wheat.

In the 19th century, grapes were grown in glasshouses known as 'vineries'. Tomatoes began to be grown as a second crop underneath the grapes, but by the 20th century had become the main crop. Between the wars, a quarter of the island's men were 'growers' or worked in the vineries or made 'chip baskets' to carry the fruit. Known as the 'love apple' then later advertised as the

'Guernsey Tom' the tomato was a symbol of the island well into the late 20th century. Competition from heavily subsidised produce of European Union countries virtually destroyed this profitable industry, but local shops and hedge stalls still sell tasty home-grown Guernsey Toms. Flowers are now the main crop grown in the island's vineries.

1 Guernsey grape growers with wicker baskets

2 Elderly Guernsey farming couple

3 Guernsey Cow in Landscape, by Denys Corbet

Before the 18th century, pigs and sheep were the most common domestic animals to be seen in Guernsey. The familiar, friendly-faced Guernsey cow only emerged during the 19th century as a special breed. It was decided in 1819 that the breed must be protected and it is today the only breed whose cows can be reared in Guernsey. The Guernsey cow yields less milk than big modern dairy breeds, but that milk is rich and produces a famously yellow butter which was once exported to England. After the Great War, dairy farmers found it difficult to make profits and the industry began to decline. Now competing with cheaper dairy produce from New Zealand and the EU, Guernsey milk, butter and cheese is rarely exported, but can be enjoyed by locals and tourists.

The Guernsey Folk & Costume Museum at Saumarez Park has excellent exhibitions on the island's rural past.

THE OCCUPATION 1940 - 45

British and French armies fighting Nazi Germany suffered a stunning defeat in May 1940. France surrendered to the Germans and was occupied by their armies, allowing Luftwaffe aircraft to set up bases on the French coasts. This meant that the Channel Islands could not be defended, so British troops withdrew and the islands were 'de-militarised'. This became clear to the enemy too late to prevent an attack by Luftwaffe bombers on St Peter Port harbour on 28 June. The 34 people killed are commemorated by a monument on the White Rock.

All but a handful of people from Alderney were evacuated to England, plus 17,000 people from Guernsey, leaving 25,000 behind. The German army drew up plans for an invasion of the islands, but on June 30th, a pilot from the Luftwaffe landed his plane at Guernsey airport and found that the island really was undefended. Guernsey surrendered to the invaders on the following day.

For the rest of the war, the islands were occupied by the enemy. Armed resistance was out of the question in such a small place, when there was one soldier for every two islanders. Those who dared defy the Germans were sent to prison camps and three Jewish women were taken away by the Nazis, meeting their deaths at Auschwitz. Two Guernsey-born soldiers sent here to spy only just avoided being shot when the German commander von Schmettow decided they should instead be treated as prisoners of war. Radios were confiscated and people were banned from going on the beaches. Fishing boats could only go out with a guard aboard to stop the men escaping. Guernsey however escaped most of the cruelty and destruction suffered by other countries in Europe. Adolf Hitler wanted to use the Occupation of the Channel Islands to show the British people how civilised the Germans could be. Some soldiers were relieved to be in a place where there was no fighting and some even came back after the war was over.

The Germans were determined that the British would not recapture the Channel Islands, so brought in up to 37,000 soldiers with artillery, aircraft, ships and tanks. They ringed the island with concrete bunkers, trenches, towers and artillery positions - some of which can still be visited. Slave labourers from Russia, occupied Europe and even Africa were used to build these fortifications and many died of ill-treatment. The fortifications were however never needed. The British only launched a few small attacks on the islands using commandos

May 9th - Liberation Day

1 German built observation tower at Pleinmont

2 German troops in St Martins

3 German troops marching in St Peter Port

and bombers, mainly aimed at annoying the Germans and finding out information. A big invasion was planned, but fortunately never carried out as Guernsey would have been left in ruins and lots of its people killed.

During 1942 and 1943, some 2,000 Channel Islanders were deported to camps in Germany. Guernsey deportees mainly went to Biberach, and sat out the war behind barbed wire. For the people left behind, things became darker as the war dragged on. Everyday things like bicycle tyres and children's toys were impossible to find. Food became in short supply and the crime rate increased. In June 1944, the Allies invaded Normandy and began to recapture

France. From that point on the Germans in the island were cut off, as was the supply of food, coal and medicines. In the winter that followed, both the islanders and the occupiers were close to starvation, even eating seaweed. Only the arrival of Red Cross food parcels on board the ship 'Vega' saved them.

On 8th May 1945 the war in Europe ended and the British sent HMS Bulldog to Guernsey to receive the surrender of the German forces. On May 9th, British soldiers from 'Force 135' landed and took back control of the island. The Occupation holds an important place in the minds of islanders and May 9th is now celebrated as Liberation Day.

TOURISTS AND INCOMERS

© D. M. Scowen

In the first half of the 19th century, many retired English people moved to Guernsey, where it was cheap to live. Others, especially Irish, came seeking jobs. By 1850, a quarter of the population was incomers. The introduction of steamships, which connected to the railways in England, led to the steady increase in tourists and a guidebook was published in 1833. The island's first tourists were the affluent middle classes but by the early 20th century a proper tourist industry had developed.

Just before the Second World War, a new airport was constructed, but it was after the war that the industry saw a major boom. Hotels were built and houses converted to guest houses to meet the demand and tourism came to employ a quarter of the workforce. Warmer than England, with stunning beaches and a flavour of France, the island became a popular destination in the years when few Britons took holidays abroad. The tourist boom was encouraged by 'duty free' watches, tobacco and alcohol. One tourist in six now comes from Europe, especially France.

Over the centuries, many French men and women travelled to Guernsey for seasonal work and some settled here. Dutch growers brought their skills to the vineries and Italians came to work in the tourist trade. In the 1980s, workers from Madeira and Portugal came to work in horticulture and tourism. The finance industry needed lawyers, accountants and bankers and brought them in from across the world, particularly from South Africa and Commonwealth countries. In the early 21st century, workers were invited over from Latvia, especially to fill jobs in restaurants and hotels.

1 British Rail passenger ferry *Sarnia*, 1962

2 Airport terminal building during construction, March 1939

3 Beautiful beaches have attracted tourists to Guernsey

People still come to live here to protect their wealth from high taxes such as death duty, which is not charged in Guernsey. These have included artists and entertainers, such as the actor Oliver Reed and thriller writer Desmond Bagley. Once known as 'rentiers', they bring money into the island's shops, restaurants and businesses. To stop the whole island being bought up by rich people, since 1965 non-locals have not been allowed to buy 'local market' houses and can only buy one of a small number of 'open market' houses which can be three times as expensive. Key workers can still however come to live here on a 'licence'.

INTERNATIONAL
FINANCE

Banks have operated in Guernsey since the eighteenth century and The Guernsey Savings Bank was founded in 1822 at the suggestion of Admiral Saumarez. It was not until 1963 however that Kleinwort Benson became the first 'merchant bank' to establish an office in the island in modern times. Business boomed and by 2008 close to 50 banks and almost 1,000 investment funds were based in Guernsey, plus trust companies, stockbrokers and insurance companies. Guernsey's finance industry was so successful that by the start of the 21st century it created almost two-thirds of the island's wealth and employed a quarter of the workforce.

Over the years Guernsey has been able to charge lower duties and taxes than elsewhere. Keiller's Marmalade was made here between 1857 and 1879 to escape the duties on sugar and to keep their recipes secret. Guernsey's simple tax rules also make it a good place to base investment schemes such as unit trusts. Tax is however no longer the main reason finance companies come here. As a small island, Guernsey is able to write laws that encourage business and can do this quickly when new ideas arise. Companies based in London, New York or other major financial centres therefore find it useful to have offices in the island.

'Captive insurance companies' have been set up here by 40% of the top 100 UK companies to help reduce their insurance costs.

Professionals such as engineers who go to work abroad can send their wages here, so they can be invested safely for the time when they return to their home country. Wealthy people with complicated lives can have savings, investments and even their houses looked after by stockbrokers or trust companies. Famous people can also have their privacy protected in this way. Occasionally, hostile newspaper or TV articles call Guernsey a 'tax haven'. However, contrary to outdated beliefs, people are not allowed to hide their money in Guernsey in order to evade taxes they are legally obliged to pay to another government.

1

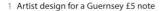

1 Artist design for a Guernsey £5 note

2 St Peter Port land mark building, Lloyds TSB Bank St Peter Port

2

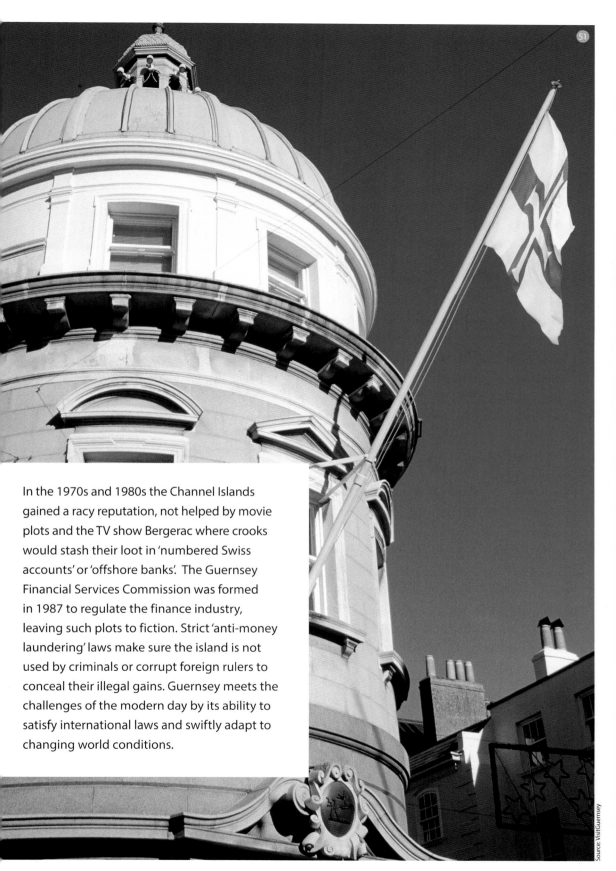

In the 1970s and 1980s the Channel Islands gained a racy reputation, not helped by movie plots and the TV show Bergerac where crooks would stash their loot in 'numbered Swiss accounts' or 'offshore banks'. The Guernsey Financial Services Commission was formed in 1987 to regulate the finance industry, leaving such plots to fiction. Strict 'anti-money laundering' laws make sure the island is not used by criminals or corrupt foreign rulers to conceal their illegal gains. Guernsey meets the challenges of the modern day by its ability to satisfy international laws and swiftly adapt to changing world conditions.

MODERN GUERNSEY

Guernesiais is rarely spoken in the modern High Street. The privateers, free trading merchants and woollen workers are people of the past. Most quarries are now landfill sites or reservoirs and there is no longer great profit in growing tomatoes or breeding Guernsey cows. Time has moved on and international finance has brought new industries to replace the old. Hotels and tourist attractions continue to compete against cheap package holidays abroad and fishermen still brave the seas for bass, crabs, scallops and lobsters despite competition from big French and British trawlers.

office blocks of St Peter Port, the traffic in the narrow lanes and the building of ever more houses on our open spaces. The rewards of prosperity can however be seen in the high standard of health care, education and general affluence. Modern Guernsey has little unemployment, crime or poverty compared to the UK. It is a safe, happy, place to live.

The islands constantly have to invent new ways of making a living. Internet gambling took off as a regulated modern business based in Alderney, whereas Guernsey became a base for packaging small value goods such as compact discs which can be sold into the EU free of VAT. Guernsey became the base of the Channel Islands' Stock Exchange in 1998 and a new Company Registry was set up in 2008 for the 17,000 Guernsey-registered companies. In the early 21st century, Intellectual Property became just the latest source of new business.

Recent prosperity has come at a price, with even Local Market homes being relatively expensive. Many people dislike the modern

GUERNSEY MUSEUM & ART GALLERY

Opened in 1979, the Museum brought together exhibits formerly in the Candie, Lukis & Island and Guille-Allès Museums. It includes collections donated by Wilfred Carey and others.

a safe, happy, place to live!